Sunflowers

Sunflowers

Growing, Cooking, and Crafting

with the
Sunniest of Plants

Diane Morey Sitton

GRAMERCY BOOKS
NEW YORK

This 2000 edition is published by Gramercy Books™, an imprint of Random House Value Publishing, Inc. 201 East 50th Street, New York, N.Y. 10022 by arrangement with Gibbs Smith, Publisher, Layton, Utah

Gramercy™ Books and design are trademarks of Random House Value Publishing, Inc.

Random House
New York • Toronto • London • Sydney • Auckland
http://www.randomhouse.com/

Printed and bound in the United States of America.

A CIP catalog record for this book is available from the Library of Congress

0-517-19463-5

Jacket design by Gus Papadopoulos

9 8 7 6 5 4 3 2 1

Contents

Acknowledgments

Gardeners and plant lovers are by nature generous, sharing people, quick to offer cuttings, seeds, and bits of wisdom gleaned from digging in the dirt and nurturing plants. Whether celebrating successes or pondering near-successes, they are as optimistic and endearing as sunflowers themselves.

I would like to thank the following for their contributions to this book:

James Sitton, my husband, for his ideas, support, and willingness to give over the garden—at least temporarily—to sunflowers.

Dub and Patty Buckner, owners of TLC Nursery, who dotted their landscape with sunflowers, providing the setting for several photographs.

Virgie Frazier, who works magic with dried herbs, flowers, and wildings.

Marge Harris, whose eye for color and design expresses itself equally in fabric or on canvas.

Dee Gibson, whose love of plants extends from the garden to the kitchen to the craft room.

Ann Sturrock, a valued neighbor who made room in her garden for sunflowers.

Spencer Morey, my father, who captured the glow of a sunflower in stained glass.

Richard Schweers, a commercial sunflower farmer, who shared of his fields and his expertise.

Heritage Village Museum, Woodville, Texas, a place of history and hospitality, and the setting for several photographs.

I would also like to acknowledge the following for their assistance in providing information: Loyd Coonrod, U.S.D.A.; Dr. Travis Miller, Texas A & M University; Joe Seals, Park Seed Co.; Wayne Scholtz and other agents with the Texas Agricultural Extension Service.

Special appreciation goes to the people whose sunflower-filled gardens I captured on film. The beauty and individuality of each garden is sure to bring inspiration and delight to readers.

Sunflowers in History

Sunflowers, with their perky dispositions and tenacious spirits, are as American as baseball and apple pie. Whether lined up at the edge of vegetable gardens or along abandoned fence rows, they gladden the heart and brighten the soul.

True to their American heritage, common sunflowers are adaptable, possessing the ability to sink their roots and find sustenance in whatever terrain nature has to offer. And where there are sunflowers, there are the hum of bees and the footprints of animals, lured to the nourishments found in the flower heads.

The sunflower's ability to endure goes back to antiquity. Carbon dating has established seeds of this strong-rooted herb in clay vessels over 3,000 years old in North America. Native Americans valued sunflowers before corn and beans were brought from the temperate climes of Central and South America.

The Sunflower

Eagle of flowers! I see thee stand,
*   And on the sun's noon-glory gaze;*
With eye like his, thy lids expand,
*   And fringe their disk with golden rays:*
Though fix'd on earth, in darkness rooted there,
Light is thine element, thy dwelling air,
*   Thy prospect heaven.*

JAMES MONTGOMERY

The common sunflower has changed little over the ages. Its fresh, bright color mimics sunlight itself, and it has a habit of turning its head to follow the sun as if to share in the celestial journey. This mannerism, instilled over eons, earned the genus the botanical name *Helianthus*, a word derived from *helios*, meaning sun, and *anthos*, meaning flower.

The most significant members of this lanky, coarse family are a throng of fast-growing annual species that originally dotted the landscape from the Great Plains to California. Like modern gardeners who choose one variety of tomato for salads, another variety for canning, and yet another variety for juice, Native Americans came to know which type of sunflower yielded the best oilseed, which type the finest flour, and which type the most flavorful snack. They especially valued a tall, single-stalked, single-flowered selection for its large seedhead.

Seed for Thought

In early Native American culture, the sunflower was a religious symbol, merging with the sun in sacred and decorative motifs.

8

Besides eating the seeds whole, native peoples of the American plains ground the small kernels into meal and flour by first parching them and then pounding them between smooth stones. They blended the coarse meal—most likely a mixture of seedmeats and hulls—with buffalo marrow and then baked it into small cakes. Sometimes these early cooks stirred the meal into soups; other times they stirred it into water and offered it as a tonic, much the same way food supplements are taken today.

The association of Native Americans with sunflowers extended beyond their use of the plant as a foodstuff. In their primitive kitchens they boiled the seedheads to extract oil, which they used to grease their hair. From the fuzzy stalks and leaves they decocted a yellow tincture; from the seeds, black and purple dyes for clothes and basketry.

In their resourceful hands a mix of roots—including the roots of sunflowers—became medicine for snakebites and rheumatism. They relied on sunflower poultices to heal burns; they used roots in medicinal teas and washes.

Pioneers, who grew sunflowers in their vegetable gardens along with corn and beans, were as resourceful as the Native Americans in utilizing each part of this bounteous plant. After harvesting the immense seedheads, they gathered the dry stalks, broke them into sections, and stacked the brittle plant material to use as kindling or fire starter. They scattered the seeds—a valuable egg-producing ration—to eager hens. They fed the leaves to cattle.

9

Sunflowers Cross the Atlantic

In the early 1500s, sunflowers made their debut in Europe, carried there as gifts from the New World by Spanish settlers returning to their homeland. Seeing the flower's resemblance to chamomile and daisies, horticulturists at the Madrid Botanic Garden planted the seed, impressed by the sunflower's beauty rather than its usefulness.

By 1557, sunflowers were so well known in Europe that Dodoens described them in *Historie of Plantes.* The illustration that accompanied his writings, a woodcut of a large, single-flowered plant with a robust stalk and substantial foliage, appeared again in 1597 in Gerard's *Herball.*

Twenty years after Dodoens introduced sunflowers in print, Nicholas Monardes included them in *Joyfull Newes out of the Newe Founde Worlde.* In describing "The Hearbe of the Sunne," he wrote:

> *This is a notable hearbe, and although that now they sent mee the seede of it, yet some yeres past wee have had it here, it is a straunge flower, for it casteth out the greatest flowers, and the moste perticulars that ever hath been seen, for it is greater then a great Platter or Dishe, the whiche hath divers coulers. It is needefull that it leane to some thyng, where it groweth, or elles it will bee alwaies falling: The seede of it is like to the seedes of a Mellon, sumwhat greater, his flower doth tourne it selfe continually towards the Sunne, and for this they call it of his name, the whiche many other flowers and hearbes do the like, it showeth marveilous faire in Gardines.*

Seed for Thought

In the language of flowers, the sunflower is the birthday flower for June 30. It symbolizes adoration, affection, constancy, false riches, glory, gratitude, and infatuation.

Sinking Their Roots in Russian Soil

Sunflowers found an advocate in Peter the Great, the Russian czar who ruled in the early 1700s. He was so impressed with the sunflowers he saw while visiting Holland that he obtained seeds. Initially, horticulturists at the St. Petersburg Botanic Garden grew sunflowers experimentally. Soon, farmers in central Russia, blessed with rich, black soil, began producing larger and healthier plants, some reaching fifteen feet tall.

By the mid-1700s, sunflower seeds had found their way to the snack trays of Russian hostesses and into the pockets of Russian children. Aawareness of the exceptional quality of the pressed oil secured the sunflower's position in Russia.

In 1835, a progressive farmer in the Ukraine plowed up his rich land and sowed sunflower seeds, creating the first commercial sunflower plantation in his country. Within the next twenty years *podsolnechniks,* as sunflowers are known in Russia, dotted the waste areas of central and south Russia, the Ukraine, and parts of Siberia. Today, sunflowers are prominent in Russia as a source of beauty, food, and medicine.

In parts of Europe snackers reach for sunflower seeds the way Americans reach for peanuts. There, sunflowers are a valuable and useful plant, providing leaves for smoking, flower buds for salads, flowers for dyestuff, and oil for cooking. In parts of Asia, manufacturers use sunflower oil as a packing agent for canned fish and as a carrier for the pigment in paint. They process the fibrous stalks into paper and burn the oil in oil lamps. In many countries oil-cake, a byproduct of sunflower oil production, is an important livestock food, fed to cows, sheep, pigs, pigeons, rabbits, and poultry.

Folk medicine throughout the world relies on the oil-laden seeds for coughs and teas made from stem parts for fevers. Russians cut the bloom-heads into chunks, mix the plantstuff with soap chips and vodka, and set this unusual mixture in the sun for nine days. They rub the potent liniment on areas of the body plagued with rheumatism.

Seed for Thought

Sunflowers are the national flower of Russia.

Of the many plants originating in what is now the United States, the sunflower is the only one with global significance as a commercial plant. From its modest beginning as a prairie wilding, the sunflower has grown to be one of the world's leading oilseed crops, second only to soybeans in importance.

Farmers in the United States began growing sunflowers commercially after World War II. The states with the highest output cut a swath through the center of the country and include North Dakota, South Dakota, Minnesota, Kansas, and Texas. The area that comprises the former Soviet Union boasts the largest number of acres in the world under cultivation with sunflowers, outranking Argentina, the second largest producer, by roughly two-and-one-half times the acreage.

The commercial crop consists of two seed types: confection and oilseeds. The large, gray-striped confection seeds make up twenty-five percent of sun-

flower production. These delicious morsels find their way into baked goods, trail mixes, granola, and cereal. Like other edibles, they are graded by size. The largest, most flawless seeds are packaged whole for snacking. Medium-sized seeds are hulled and sold roasted or raw. The smallest seeds are left in-shell and are earmarked for birdseed.

Oilseed varieties make up seventy-five percent of the trade. Each year, growers worldwide produce more than five million metric tons of the small, black seeds. The best varieties, developed by Russian researchers, contain fifty percent oil.

The citron-yellow oil pressed from these oil-type sunflower seeds is premium quality, low in saturated fats and high in polyunsaturated fats. Its clean, sweet taste and high smoking point contribute to its marketability. It is an ingredient in margarines, soaps, and cosmetics. The oilseed varieties are also marketed as wild bird food.

Seed for Thought

*The French word for sunflower
is* tournesol, *or literally
"turn with the sun."*

Sunflowers in the Garden

The windflower and the violet, they
perished long ago.
And the brier-rose and the orchis
died amid the summer glow;
But on the hill the golden-rod,
and the aster in the wood,
And the yellow sunflower by the
brook, in autumn beauty stood,
Till fell the frost from the clear
cold heaven, as fall the plague of men,
And the brightness of their smile
was gone from upland, glade and glen.

FROM "THE DEATH OF THE FLOWERS"
WILLIAM CULLEN BRYANT

In nature's garden, there exist approximately 150 species of sunflowers. These robust plants that make up the genus *Helianthus* grow throughout the United States, thriving in an assortment of habitats including grassy plains, sandy woodlands, and moist bottomlands. They invade ditches, swales, and depressions; they thrive in hostile terrain, including the rocky, chemical-laden fringe of railroad tracks.

Typically, the rough, hairy stalks of these sun-loving natives stretch three to ten feet tall. A single glorious flower crowns some types; a profusion of blooms decorates others. Whether single or multiple, the blooms are actually flattened disks made up of hundreds of tiny, tubular flowers. The large, colorful petals that surround the disk are sterile "ray" flowers. Because each bloom is a multiple flower, sunflowers belong to the daisy family, *Compositae*.

17

New Faces for New Places

few garden flowers delight the eye as much as sunflowers. Although most gardeners think of gigantic, nodding seedheads, an array of cultivars offers growers a wide selection when choosing height, color, and decorative value.

One of the most eye-catching offerings from the test plots and imaginations of plant breeders are the dwarf-sized sunflowers that grow two feet tall or less. Instead of being assigned to the back of the garden—like their full-sized cousins that grow eight or even fifteen feet tall—these Lilliputian cultivars demand to be lined up in front of borders and in front of taller-growing annuals.

Thanks, too, to the magic of science, the size of sunflower blooms is not dependent on the size of sunflower plants. Today, disks the size of dinner plates spring from squatty plants as well as tall plants, and diminutive flowers decorate tall varieties as well as short varieties.

Besides an ever-increasing range of size, sunflowers dazzle gardeners with a broadening spectrum of color. Not only do flowers imitate the sun with all hues of yellows and golds, but blooms look to the earth for shades of bronze, mahogany, purple, and orange. Some varieties offer two colors, splashed on the flower in concentric rings radiating outward from the center.

Pollenless sunflowers, a gift from science to gardeners who enjoy growing flowers for cutting, are sterile and do not set seed. Not only are the blooms litter-free — void of pollen that can stain clothing and tablecloths — but they are medium-sized, making them manageable in bouquets.

Seed for Thought

Scientists use the word "heliatropic"
to refer to the ability of sunflower blooms to
face the sun from morning till night.

Versatile and Useful

The number of varieties attests to the plant's versatility and usefulness. The traditional sunflower, with its towering height, thick stalk, sizable foliage, and massive flower, grows into a living screen, providing privacy. Use these gentle giants to create a garden room or a secret garden for children. Plant them next to a medium-sized fence and watch them grow. The fence softens their "legginess"; the flowers add spectacular height. Large varieties lined up in a row or sowed in a block help to camouflage unattractive areas, including trash stations and toolsheds.

On the other hand, tall-growing cultivars can be a dramatic device to attract attention. Use them to encircle a gazebo or flagpost. Plant them at each corner of a cedar arbor.

Tall varieties, when planted in the row two weeks before runner beans, cucumbers, gourds, or other vining crops, act as a living trellis, keeping the harvest off the ground. Not only do the vegetables stay clean, but they grow and develop within arm's reach, making them easy to pick.

Mid-size varieties add height to flower gardens while complementing zinnias, marigolds, and other brightly colored summer annuals. Line them up in colorful rows along white picket fences.

Short cultivars provide splashes of color along walkways and small fences. Use them to encircle a birdbath, or plant them at the base of a mailbox or lightpost. Their petite stature adapts well to pots or planters positioned on sunny decks or patios.

Sunflowers of any height bring excitement and educational value to children's gardens. From the moment the robust seedlings pop out of the soil to the day when the seedheads are cut, there are lessons to be learned from Mother Nature. And the fun for kids doesn't stop in summer; in winter they will delight in offering the fruits of their labor to hungry birds.

Seed for Thought

At one time people grew sunflowers near their homes as a protection against malaria. The practice may have been reinforced by the fact that sunflower blooms have insecticidal properties.

Meeting Their Needs

Sunflowers are among the easiest flowers to grow. But unlike their wilding relatives that thrive on neglect, cultivated varieties appreciate some care.

Although seedlings are cold resistant, sunflowers show the most vigor when the weather has stabilized and the days and nights are somewhat warm. Plant the seeds after all danger of frost is past (after frost-free date), in April or May. Choose a site in full sun. Assign tall varieties to the north side of the garden so their shadows won't fall on other crops.

Sunflowers are not particular about soil, although they appreciate well-drained, loose loam. Sow large-seeded varieties 1 inch deep and 6 inches apart. Keep the soil evenly moist until germination occurs, usually within 14 days. Thin the seedlings of large cultivars to 18 inches apart. Extend the duration of bloom of single-flowered varieties by making successive plantings one week apart.

Mulch, applied in a 3- to 4-inch layer, helps to conserve moisture and thwart weeds. Although sunflowers are drought resistant, regular, deep watering appeals to their fast-growing nature. Tall varieties are well suited to fence lines where they receive extra support. If necessary, stake plants to keep them upright. Except for an occasional occurrence of aphids or powdery mildew, sunflowers are remarkably trouble free. Some varieties bloom as early as 55 days after planting.

As the blooms of sunflowers mature, their centers change. The disks of most varieties start out as green-yellow and then turn to yellow before darkening to brown. Pollen and seed development account for the deepening color. The weight of the mature seedheads of large varieties causes the stems to bend, giving the plants a somber, bowed appearance.

It is not unusual to see squirrels—delighted with the ripening bounty—climb the stalks and then ride the seedheads to the ground where they devour the nutlike morsels. Birds, too, flock to the cache. To prevent ravenous wildlife from stealing the crop as it develops, cover the seedheads with paper sacks, mesh bags, burlap bags, cheesecloth, pantyhose, or other permeable material.

If the weather is warm and dry and if wildlife isn't a problem, allow the seeds to ripen naturally in the garden. Cut the seedheads when they are about to shed their crop.

Otherwise, harvest the seedheads when the seeds start to turn brown or when the backs of the seedheads turn yellow. Cut the seed-laden disks, leaving at least two feet of stem attached, and hang them upside down in a dry, airy place such as a well-ventilated garage or screened-in porch. In basements or other areas with poor air flow, mold sometimes forms on the heavy seedheads. If you must use this kind of location, use a fan to improve air circulation.

While curing, seedheads are vulnerable to squirrels, mice, chipmunks, and other determined and clever wildlife, so protect them. In four weeks or so, the stalks becomes brittle and the fibers shrink, loosening the seeds and signaling that the seedheads have cured.

At one time Russian peasants removed the seed from the heads by holding them against a spinning disk through which nails had been hammered. The loosened seeds fell into open sacks. Today's methods, while safer, are folksy and primitive as well. If pushing against them with a hard rub of the thumb doesn't extract the seeds, then rub two seedheads together, rake each seedhead with a stiff brush, or scuff the heads over a screen of 1/2-inch hardware cloth tacked over a box. If all else fails, thresh the seeds loose by placing the head in a feedsack or burlap bag and thumping it against a hard surface.

If any seeds feel moist, spread them out in a single layer in a protected, well-ventilated location until they are completely dry. For kitchen use, winnow out the chaff and then store the dry seeds in air-tight containers.

Seed for Thought

An old Tewa Nation song says that sunflowers are watered by the tears of Navajo girls.

Varieties with flair

There is a sunflower for almost every garden, no matter how big or small. In fact, their wide range of sizes, colors, and habits makes it possible to include several varieties of sunflowers in the landscape.

Sungold. It is so thickly petaled that at first glance this double sunflower appears to be a chrysanthemum. The quilled flowers often reach 5 inches across, showering gardens and bouquets with their golden beauty. Plants grow to six feet tall and produce an abundance of blooms.

A dwarf variety, **Teddy Bear**, has the same sensational flowers on plants that grow to 3 feet tall. Mix either variety in a border with marigolds to create a summer glow.

Autumn Beauty. The profusion of rusty bronze, deep burgundy, golden yellow, and mahogany red flowers makes this tall grower a candidate for almost every garden. Each 6-to-8-foot, multi-branching plant produces many bicolored, dark-centered blooms that are perfect for brightening arrangements or for accenting the back of the border from mid- to late-summer.

Seed for Thought

Bees love sunflowers. Early gardeners planted sunflowers among their runner beans to increase pollination.

Mammoth Russian. This traditional sunflower reaches 10 or more feet tall, producing one enormous yellow flower at the top of the thick stem. The bloom typically stretches a foot wide, large enough to hold 1,000 or more gray-and-white-striped seeds as a mature seedhead. Besides the bounty of seeds to roast or feed to birds, the seedheads themselves are often included in harvest arrangements. This is a reliable performer; grow it to meet the challenge of a competitive neighbor.

Other varieties with almost identical characteristics are marketed under various names, including **Giant Greystripe, Russian Giant,** and **Giganteus.**

Sunspot

Sunbeam

Sunspot. With its classic, 10-inch nodding heads poised atop compact, 2-foot-tall plants, this variety appeals to children as well as to the child in every adult. Flowers, rimmed with bright yellow petals, appear just 60 days after planting. The golden brown centers are a stockpile of seeds.

Sunbeam. This pollenless cultivar earns a place in the cutting garden or border for its large, long-lasting flowers. Each bloom crowns the top of a strong, single stem, making them easy to cut and arrange in bouquets. Flowers feature green centers surrounded by golden yellow ray petals. The centers darken as the flowers mature. Plants reach 5 feet tall and reward eager gardeners with blooms within 60 to 65 days after planting.

Valentine. Buttery yellow blooms with fibrous black centers make this variety an asset for beds and borders. Cut the 6-inch flowers as they come into bud and watch them open in bouquets. With cut-flower food they last more than two weeks. Plants reach 5 feet tall.

Velvet Queen. This regal-looking beauty decorates its surroundings with deep burgundy blooms made more majestic by their imposingly dark centers. The well-branched, free-flowering plants stand 6 feet tall. The medium-sized blooms are striking in borders and cut bouquets.

Maximilian. In the wild, prairie sunflower, as it is sometimes called, grows from Texas northward through the Central Plains. It is an adaptable perennial, well suited to native gardens and fence lines. Its abundant supply of seeds attracts many species of birds, making it an asset in wildlife gardens. This hardy sunflower grows in almost any soil but requires full sun to reach its 8-foot, bloom-laden potential. To share plants with friends, lift and divide established clumps in fall.

Seed for Thought

The word sunflower *existed in England before the introduction of the common sunflower. Through history the name has been shared by calendula, chrysanthemum, elecampane, marigold, and several other plants whose flowers tend to face the sun.*

Piccolo. It doesn't take many plants of this variety to fill a bed or border with color. Each branching, 4-foot-tall plant produces a multitude of miniature blooms. With their golden petals and dark centers, these 4-inch sunflowers add cheerful accents to beds, borders, and bouquets.

Jerusalem Artichoke. Although it produces clusters of small, yellow flowers at the tops of its 10-foot-tall stalks, this sunflower is valued for the sweet tubers that it develops underground. Plant the knobby tubers 3 or 4 inches deep and 24 inches apart in spring or fall in a sunny location in well-drained soil. Either obtain them from seed companies, purchase the ones in the produce section of the supermarket, or plant tubers saved from a previous harvest. They sprout in 2 to 3 weeks. The harvest begins about 100 days after planting.

It's All in a Name

Jerusalem artichoke is neither an artichoke nor is it from Jerusalem. The misleading moniker came about after explorers to the New World carried this robust member of the sunflower family back to their European homeland in 1616. The French called the plant artichauts du Canada *because the flavor of the tasty tubers resembled artichokes.*

The Italians dubbed the plant Girasole, *which means "turning toward the sun." To the British, who imported the plant from Italy, the word sounded like Jerusalem. European botanists classified it as* Helianthus tuberosus, *a descriptive name meaning "tuberous sunflower."*

Today, growers sometimes market these increasingly popular vegetables as "sunchokes."

Sunflowers Measure Up

- The tallest sunflower plant on record stretched 25 feet, 5 1/2 inches tall. It was grown in the Netherlands.

- The largest sunflower head on record measured 32 1/2 inches in diameter. It was grown in Canada.

- The shortest fully mature sunflower on record was 2.2 inches tall. It was grown in Oregon, using the bonsai technique.

GUINNESS BOOK OF WORLD RECORDS

Bigger Is Better

Gardeners of all ages enjoy growing BIG sunflowers. To get a head start on a new record, follow these steps.

1. Buy seeds of the largest variety available. (Mammoth types are good record-breakers.)

2. Give each plant plenty of growing space in full sun.

3. Sow the seeds in moderately fertile, well-drained loam.

4. Stake the plants with sturdy poles to provide extra support. Position the stakes at the time of planting to avoid injuring the tender roots.

5. Keep the plants thriving with ample water and food.

6. Pinch off any lateral shoots that form.

Keep a ladder and tape measure handy to confirm the results, or document your record-breaker on film.

Sunflowers In the Kitchen

Sunflower seeds, with their nutlike taste and nutritional benefits, not only make a flavorful snack but can be incorporated into a variety of foodstuffs including breads, cookies, and salads. For the highest yield of seeds per plant, select giant-headed varieties, like Mammoth Russian.

Compared to many snack foods, sunflower kernels are a storehouse of nutrition. They contain over a dozen vitamins and minerals, including a generous supply of B vitamins, vitamin A, potassium, and phosphorus. Each minute kernel is rich in iron, power-packed with 25 percent protein, and cholesterol-free. The fiber content of three tablespoons of sunflower kernels is equal to a serving of bran-cereal flakes. One-fourth cup contains approximately 200 calories.

Photo courtesy National Garden Bureau

No, the heart that has truly lov'd never forgets,
But as truly loves on to the close,
As the sunflower turns on her god, when he sets,
The same look which she turn'd when he rose.

FROM "Believe Me, If All Those Endearing Young Charms"
THOMAS MOORE

34

Seed for Thought

Some health food enthusiasts refer to sunflower seed sprouts as "sunflower lettuce."

Roasted Seeds

The simplest way to prepare sunflowers seeds for snacking is by roasting them whole. Begin by soaking unhulled seeds in water for 8 hours. For a salty flavor, submerge them in brine. After letting them soak, drain the water, spread the seeds on a shallow baking sheet, and roast at 200 degrees Fahrenheit for 3 hours or until crisp. Occasionally stir the seeds during cooking.

Sunflower Seed Sprouts

The sprouts of unhulled sunflower seeds may be incorporated into the menu as a vitamin-rich vegetable in salads or sandwiches. Sprouting is fast, easy, and does not depend on the season or the weather. Avoid using chemically treated seeds.

Sprouting in water. Like other seeds and grains, sunflower seeds increase their volume during the sprouting process. Usually, 1/2 cup is sufficient per batch.

Prepare unhulled, raw sunflower seeds by soaking them overnight to soften the seed case. Drain the water off the seeds and then place them in a glass jar with cheesecloth or nylon netting held in place over the opening with a string or rubber band. Rinse the seeds and then set the jar at an angle upside-down in a bowl so that the excess water continues to drain.

Place the jar and bowl in a moderately cool cabinet (70 degrees F.), out of bright light. Too much light causes the seeds to dry out; too high a temperature causes mold; too low a temperature inhibits sprouting.

Rinse the sprouts in the morning and evening, each time repositioning the jar in its tilted, upside-down position. Sunflower seeds can require several days to sprout.

Sprouting in soil. Sunflower seeds sprouted by this technique yield taller shoots than those sprouted in water. Each shoot has two green leaves. Sprouts generated in soil require 10 days to 2 weeks.

First, soak 1/2 cup of unhulled raw sunflower seeds in water overnight. Poke drainage holes in a 9- by 13-inch foil pan before filling it with a 1-inch layer of potting soil. Drain the seeds before scattering them evenly over the soil. Cover them with an additional 1/4-inch layer of soil, pressed firmly down. Next, blanket the sprout garden with dampened newspaper. Place the foil pan on a cookie sheet to catch any water that drains from the bottom.

Keep the soil moist until germination, watering daily if necessary. Emergence of the seedling is a signal for more light. Remove the newspaper and place the pan near a sunny window or on a bright porch. Keep the soil evenly moist to promote strong growth. Pluck off the hulls from the tender new growth.

Harvest sunflower sprouts when the first two leaves unfurl and turn green. Cut the delicate shoots above the soil line, rinse them in cold water, and then drain. Sprouts retain their freshness for up to two weeks when stored in the refrigerator in plastic bags lined with paper towels.

How to Remove Seedmeats from Hulls

In order to use sunflower seeds in most recipes, it is first necessary to remove the flavorful raw seedmeats from the hulls. Techniques vary from placing the seeds in a heavy plastic bag and bursting them open with a rolling pin to spinning them in a blender. After either procedure, retrieve the tasty seedmeats by dumping the cracked mixture into a pan of water, stirring it slowly, and then allowing it to settle. The heavy kernels sink to the bottom; the hulls float to the surface. Prehulled seeds for roasting and recipes are available in bulk at health food stores.

Although sunflower kernels can be eaten raw, roasting them brings out their nutlike flavor. Simply spread the seedmeats in a single layer on a cookie sheet and cook them slowly in a moderately warm oven (250 degrees F.) until they turn from greenish beige to golden brown. Use them unseasoned as a replacement for nuts in banana bread, date-nut bread, or cookie recipes.

Besides being used whole to add flavor and texture, roasted seedmeats can be ground into a flour. Use this flavor-filled and nutritious powder to replace part of the flour called for in cookies, pancakes, or muffins. Stir it into soups or stews as a thickening agent.

Eat toasted sunflower kernels plain or sprinkled with salt as a snack. Create a spicy treat by dusting them lightly with chili powder or Cajun seasoning. Roast them into delicious tidbits resembling commercially prepared snacks by combining 3 tablespoons of oil and 3 tablespoons of soy sauce (or Worcestershire sauce) in a shallow pan. Add one pound of hulled sunflower seeds, tossing them until they are well coated with the mixture. Bake at 250 degrees F. until they are done. Stir them occasionally as they cook. When they have cooled to room temperature, put them in sealed plastic bags or tightly closed jars. Keep them fresh by storing them in the refrigerator.

Jerusalem Artichokes

In the kitchen, the gnarled tubers of this sunflower are surprisingly versatile. When raw, the translucent flesh has a crunchy texture, resembling water chestnuts; when cooked it is soft and potatolike.

Enjoy its delicate flavor and distinctive texture by scattering thinly sliced pieces of raw, peeled tuber across the top of green salads or by sautéing them lightly in butter and serving them as a vegetable. Add slices or small chunks of tuber to peas, beans, or stir-fry, or simmer them lightly and then smother them with cheese sauce. Their nutty flavor complements raw mushrooms. To cook them like potatoes, simmer them for 20 minutes and then drain. Serve them smothered with herb butter.

Jerusalem artichokes are tasty with or without their thin, light tan skins. To prepare them, rinse them under running water before scrubbing them clean with a vegetable brush. If desired, peel them with a potato parer. Maintain their crunchiness for salads by storing peeled tubers in a jar of water in the refrigerator. They contain 120 calories per cup and are rich in iron and low in sodium.

Seed for Thought

Jerusalem artichokes grew in eastern North America, where they were eaten by Native Americans long before the discovery of America.

Sunshine Snack Mix

1/2 cup coarsely chopped walnuts

1/2 cup roasted, salted sunflower seed kernels

1/2 cup raisins

1/2 cup unsweetened, flaked coconut

1/2 cup chopped dates

1/2 cup chopped dried peaches

Measure all ingredients and toss in a large bowl. Pour into jars or plastic containers. Cover tightly and refrigerate. Yield: 3 1/2 cups.

Seed for Thought

Bees make a delicious amber honey from sunflowers.

Gold Nuggets

8 ounces dried apricots, chopped

2 1/2 cups flaked coconut

3/4 cup sweetened condensed milk

1 cup finely chopped roasted sunflower seed kernels (unsalted)

Mix apricots, coconut, and milk in small bowl. Shape into 1-inch balls; roll each in sunflower kernels. Let stand until firm. Chill. Yield: 2 dozen.

Sunflower Herb Dip

2/3 cup plain yogurt

1/2 cup mayonnaise

2 teaspoons chives

2 teaspoons parsley flakes

1/2 teaspoon dry mustard

1/2 teaspoon garlic powder

1/4 teaspoon paprika

1/2 cup sunflower kernels

Blend in food processor until sunflower kernels are chopped. Chill overnight. Serve with crackers, chips, or raw vegetables. Yield: approximately 2 cups.

Seed for Thought

The unopened flower buds of sunflowers become a delicacy when they are simmered and served with butter to be eaten the same way as artichokes.

Sunflower Seed Garnish

4 cups raw sunflower kernels

1/2 cup grated Parmesan cheese

2 tablespoons melted butter

1/2 teaspoon salt

1/8 teaspoon garlic powder

Place all ingredients in a 2-quart jar and shake until mixed thoroughly. Bake at 350 degrees F. for 30 minutes, stirring occasionally. Cool completely. Store in a covered container and use as needed as salad garnish or casserole topping.

Yield: 4 1/2 cups.

Sunflower Bread

1 3/4 cup unsifted all-purpose flour

2/3 cup sugar

1 teaspoon ground cinnamon

1/8 teaspoon ground nutmeg

3/4 teaspoon baking powder

1/2 teaspoon baking soda

1/2 teaspoon salt (optional)

3/4 cup unsalted sunflower kernels

1/2 cup golden raisins

3 teaspoons lemon zest

1/2 cup sunflower oil

2 eggs

1 1/2 teaspoons vanilla extract

2 cups coarsely shredded zucchini

Preheat oven to 350° F. Grease and flour 8 1/2 by 4 1/2-inch loaf pan.

In mixing bowl, combine flour, sugar, spices, baking powder, baking soda, and salt. Mix remaining sunflower kernels, raisins, and lemon zest into dry ingredients.

Blend oil, eggs, and vanilla in a small bowl. Add zucchini. Stir into dry ingredients until well blended. Spread into prepared pan.

Bake 55 to 60 minutes or until toothpick inserted in center comes out clean. Garnish with sunflowers. Cool bread in pan 10 minutes. Remove from pan; cool completely on wire rack. Wrap and store overnight before slicing.
Yield: 1 loaf.

Seed for Thought

In parts of the world sunflower seeds are roasted like coffee and then brewed into a hot beverage.

45

for the Birds

Sunflowers are easy plants for gardeners to grow for birds. The seeds can be left on the lolling seedheads, attracting birds to the landscape, or they can be harvested, cured, and fed back to the birds in winter as a tempting entree or as part of a custom blend.

The group of birds known as seedeaters is especially adept at reaching the nourishing seedmeat inside the stubborn shell. Their proficiency stems from their strong, cone-shaped bills designed to crack hard, dry seeds. Cardinals, along with finches and towhees, are members of this group. Most seedeaters, while relishing a feeder full of sunflower seeds, assist gardeners by eating insects as well.

Birds Attracted to Sunflower Seeds:

American goldfinch
Blue jay
Cardinal
Chickadee
Common flicker
Common grackle
Dark-eyed junco
Dark nuthatch
Downy woodpecker
House finch
House sparrow
Mourning dove
Purple finch
Red-headed woodpecker
Scrub jay
Tufted titmouse
White-throated sparrow
White-crowned sparrow

Custom Mixes

Although bird-lovers can choose from a wide selection of birdseed mixes, many commercial blends contain a high percentage of hulled oats, milo, and other "filler" that birds ignore at feeders.

Custom mixes made at home from bulk ingredients can be tailored to whet the appetites of specific birds, resulting in little or no waste. To attract the greatest number of species, offer special blends at ground feeders and platform feeders.

Seed for Thought

In a 1914 seed catalog, Jerusalem artichokes were introduced as "Helianti," a new winter vegetable to replace asparagus.

Basic Birdseed Mix

8 cups sunflower seeds
    (unhulled black oilseed type)

5 1/2 cups millet (white proso)

2 1/2 cups cracked corn (fine or medium)

Mix all ingredients. Yield: 1 gallon

High-Energy Treat

Suet is a welcome source of quick energy to many birds, including chickadees, blue jays, and mockingbirds. The addition of sunflower seeds, berries, and breadstuffs increases its nutritional value and appeal.

Beef suet, preferred above other kinds, is inexpensive and easy to obtain from butchers. Make sure that it is fresh, firm, and white.

Suet-Sunflower Mix

4 1/2 cups ground fresh suet

3/4 cup dried, finely ground whole wheat bread or crackers

1/2 cup raw, unsalted sunflower kernels

1/4 cup millet (white proso)

1/4 cup dried, chopped berries or raisins

Melt the suet in a pan over low heat. Meanwhile, mix the remaining ingredients in a large bowl. When the suet has cooled and begins to thicken, pour it over the mixture in the bowl. Mix well. Pour or pack it into forms, suet feeders, pine cones, or short sections of log drilled with 1-inch-diameter holes.

Yield: 6 1/4 cups.

Sunflowers in the Craft Room

Ah, Sun-flower! weary of time,
Who countest the steps of the Sun;
Seeking after that sweet golden clime,
Where the traveller's journey is done
FROM *SONGS OF EXPERIENCE,* "AH! SUN-FLOWER"

WILLIAM BLAKE

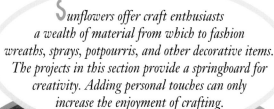

Sunflowers offer craft enthusiasts a wealth of material from which to fashion wreaths, sprays, potpourris, and other decorative items. The projects in this section provide a springboard for creativity. Adding personal touches can only increase the enjoyment of crafting.

Drying Sunflowers for Crafting

Harvesting: The blooms of small-flowered, decorative varieties, including native sun-flowers, lend themselves to crafting. The goal of drying flowers is to maintain their color and form. Sunflowers should be harvested in full, fresh color just before the peak of bloom. Harvest the flowers when they are completely dry. In summer, mid- to late-morning is an ideal time; by then the dew has evaporated but the flowers have not yet wilted from the scorching sun.

Drying Techniques: There are several techniques used to dry sunflowers and other plant material. The goal is to eliminate moisture, rendering the material the consistency of cereal flakes—dry and crisp.

Air drying is a simple technique that allows the moisture in flowers, foliage, and stems to evaporate naturally. There are two ways sunflowers can be dried by this method: they can be suspended upside down, or they can be placed flat on drying racks or newspaper. Either way, sunflowers retain the most color and dry the most successfully when put in warm, dark locations with good air flow.

Hang drying is the best technique for sunflowers harvested with long stems. If the foliage is intact, suspend each flower individually in a head-down position. If the foliage has been removed, two or three stalks may be clustered together for drying. Suitable locations include dimly lit areas with good air circulation such as utility or storage rooms where freezers or hot water heaters keep the air warm and dry.

Flowers can require seven days or more to dry, depending on the size and thickness of the stems and blooms and the temperature and humidity of the drying area. Check the flowers frequently for mildew.

Another way to air dry sunflowers is to place their flowers and petals on drying racks. The racks allow air to circulate completely around the flowers, promoting fast, even drying. Elevate an old, hole-riddled window screen between bricks, books, or other objects so that stems can hang through it, allowing the flower heads to dry face-up on top of the screen. Place flowers without stems and sunflower petals in single layers on drying screens. Turn the material every two days.

Flowers without stems and individual petals may be dried on layers of newspaper. Turn the plant material every day. If the paper shows signs of dampness, replace it.

Dehydrators are efficient, fast, and convenient to use. Position individual blooms face up in single layers with space between them. Scatter large flower petals in single layers on the drying racks, but remember: they shrink as they dry and may fall through the openings in the racks. Petals dry in as little as 12 hours; flowers require 24 hours or more.

Microwave ovens are the fastest way to dry sunflower petals, but care must be taken to avoid burning the fragile plant material. Scatter the petals in single layers between paper towels. Dry small quantities in each batch. Total drying time depends on the power of the microwave, the number of petals in each batch, and the moisture content of the petals. Experimentation with the length of drying time is usually required. When they are done, petals should feel dry and crisp. If they feel damp, reset the timer for another 15 to 30 seconds. Microwave drying is not recommended for the bulky flower heads of sunflowers.

Seed for Thought
Louis XIV, France's Sun King, used
sunflowers as a symbol of his reign.

Sunflower and field flower Spray

With their long stems and bright yellow blooms, sunflowers lend themselves to sprays. Hang this cheerful bundle of sunflowers, herbs, and field flowers on doors, walls, or posts that need brightening. It is easy to construct and economical to make. In areas with limited surface space, it is an excellent alternative to bouquets displayed in vases.

The finished spray is flat-backed to simplify hanging. Suggested length: 34 inches.

Dried Materials: Sunflowers on 30-inch stems, colicroot (*Aletris aurea*), hat pins (*Eriocaulon decangulare*), sweet Annie (*Artemisia annua*), white yarrow, or other long-stemmed herbs or wildings.

Supplies: Scissors, garden clippers, elastic band, 36-inch lengths of shredded raffia.

Directions:

1. First, assemble the dried materials, bunch by bunch, separating the stems. Do not cut the stalks until the project is completed.

2. Lay a base of sweet Annie flat on the surface of the work table with the uppermost tips of the herb higher in the center, peaking to form a triangular shape.

3. Position the sunflowers in a pleasing balance atop the sweet Annie with the largest bloom near the center of the spray. Let the sweet Annie extend approximately 4 inches from the tip of the tallest sunflower. Since the sunflower blooms are the focal point, work with an uneven number of flowers such as three, five, or seven.

4. Once the bundle begins taking shape, secure the stems with an elastic band or a piece of string. This stabilizes the arrangement during construction.

5. Create fullness and interest by adding the other dried materials. Slip a few sprigs into the heart of the spray by inserting them, stem end first, from the top. Layer shorter sprigs by laying them on top of the sunflowers. Work to create a pleasing balance.

6. Arrange the material to camouflage long stems. Add more sweet Annie on top if needed.

7. After positioning all the dried material, trim the stems evenly across the bottom using the garden clippers.

8. Tie a bow of shredded raffia approximately 10 inches from the bottom of the stems.

Seed for Thought

In 1987, Vincent van Gogh's Sunflowers
painting sold at auction for a record
$39.9 million.

Sunflower and Herb Wreath

This large, circular wreath uses vibrant yellow and gold sunflowers with herbs and wildings to create a light, airy effect. Hang it on a wall in place of a picture, or use it to brighten halls or entryways.

Substitutions for many of the fresh materials can be made using native plants abundant in different geographic locations. The fresh green materials curl and lighten as they dry.

The finished wreath measures 26 inches across. Along with the dried sunflowers, it may contain fresh or dried materials or a combination of both.

Fresh Materials: Bracken fronds, sprigs of bay foliage, sprigs of rosemary, white yarrow, silver king artemisia, sweet Annie.

Dried Materials: Sunflowers, one variety or several.

Supplies: 18-inch grapevine wreath, 36-inch lengths of raffia in three different colors (burgundy, natural, and green or as preferred), garden clippers, scissors, glue gun.

Directions:

1. Working clockwise, begin weaving sprigs of artemisia into the outside edge of the wreath form. Stick the sprigs through the grapevine until they are secure, leaving 6 to 8 inches extending beyond the edge of the wreath form. Arrange them so they radiate outward in a uniform manner.

2. Following the same procedure, add sprigs of sweet Annie, working them into the edge and body of the wreath form.

3. Fill in with bracken, covering more and more of the wreath form. Work the bracken into the grapevine until it holds.

4. Add bay and yarrow, filling in empty areas and striving toward a pleasing balance.

5. Camouflage the inside edge of the wreath form using curved sprigs of rosemary. Work in a clockwise direction. For a nonstructured look, let some sprigs extend into the center of the wreath.

6. Once the base is completed, lay the wreath flat and then position sunflowers in groups of three or five. Experiment until the arrangement is pleasing; then secure the flowers to the wreath using hot glue.

7. Make a bow out of raffia. Shred the colorful streamers for a light, airy effect. Attach it to the wreath with hot glue or tie it on with pieces of raffia.

Seed for Thought

The Navajo made crude flutes from the stalks of sunflowers.

Sunflower Hat

few things are as nostalgic as a broad-brimmed straw hat trimmed with dried herbs, flowers, and ribbon. This hat, with its sunflower, green tulle, and gingham ribbon, is a perfect fashion accent for summer picnics. When it's not being worn, hang it on an antique hat stand or a bedpost to create a vignette from the past. Display it on a table near an antique book. Show it off on a door or wall.

Materials: Straw hat; one large dried sunflower; 60 inches of 1 1/2-inch-wide ribbon for hat band and bow; cluster of dried white yarrow, baby's breath, or German statice; 4-inch by 36-inch strip of green tulle.

Supplies: Scissors, hot glue gun, pins, needle, and green thread.

Directions:

1. Cut a piece of ribbon 2 inches longer than the base of the hat's crown.

2. Position the ribbon around the base of the crown, overlapping the two ends on one side. Secure the ribbon to the hat with drops of hot glue. Join the ends with glue or by sewing them together.

3. Cut one 6-inch piece of ribbon, trimming the ends at angles. Fold it in half lengthwise. Glue the folded end to the hat band where the ribbon joins so that the ends rest across the brim of the hat, angled toward the back.

4. Fashion a flat bow out of 12 inches of ribbon. Glue it or sew it at the spot where the band joins.

5. Position sprigs of yarrow so that they radiate outward in a fan shape from the sides and top of the bow. Stick the ends underneath the ribbon. Secure them with glue.

6. Using the needle and thread, gather the tulle along one long edge. Pull it tight until it is shaped like a fan. Glue the green fan on top of the center of the bow so that it flares upward.

7. Glue the sunflower at the base of the tulle.

Seed for Thought

Sunflower chests were crafted in Connecticut in the late 17th and early 18th centuries. They featured hand-carved sunflower designs on the center front panels.

Sunshine Potpourri

This cheerful potpourri adds a ray of sunshine and a fresh fragrance to bedrooms, living rooms, entryways, and other areas that need a bright, colorful accent. Display it in cut glass containers and let the facets reflect the colors and textures, or bag it in tiny fabric pouches for sachets. Place the sachets in linen drawers or hang them from the backs of chairs.

This recipe makes approximately 1 gallon of potpourri.

Materials:

4 cups dried sunflower petals

3 cups dried cosmos flowers (yellow and orange)

3 cups dried yarrow flowers

2 cups dried lemon verbena leaves

2 cups dried lemon zest

1/2 cup whole star anise pods

1 cup whole allspice seeds

1/2 cup chopped orrisroot

1 cup gray-striped sunflower seeds

10 drops vanilla oil

10 drops lemon verbena oil

20 drops orange oil

Whole small, dried sunflower heads (optional)

Directions:

Place spices, orrisroot, and oil together in a glass jar with a tight-fitting lid. Cover and set aside for 1 week to blend; gently shake every 2 days to assure good saturation.

Combine this fragrant mixture with the remaining ingredients in a glass container with a tight-fitting lid; shake gently to mix. Set in a dark, dry place for 3 to 5 weeks to allow the fragrances to mingle.

Occasionally turn the container to promote blending.

Seed for Thought

The sunflower was officially named the state flower of Kansas in 1903.

Artwork by Marge Harris

Sunflower Stitchery

Nothing says "country" more than a calico sunflower. Display this cheerful stitchery in any room of the house, or delight a friend by giving it to him or her for a birthday or other special occasion.

The finished project measures 5 by 7 inches and has its own hanger. The directions are simple enough for beginners.

Materials: 2 pieces 5-inch by 7-inch cotton material, 1 piece 4 1/2-inch by 6 l/2-inch lightweight batting or craft fleece, 4-inch square yellow fabric, 3-inch by 4-inch piece green calico fabric, 2-inch square brown calico fabric, thread (1 green, 1 light brown), 12-inch length jute cord.

Optional: (1) Spray starch to stiffen flower and leaves to prevent fraying, or seam sealant to seal edges. (2) White glue to attach pieces instead of sewing them.

Order of application:

1. Fringe front and back pieces about 3/16 inch on edges. Sandwich all three pieces (front, back, batting). Pin.

2. Finger-press edges of front in about 3/4 inch to 1 inch. This will help to provide a straight quilting line for the quilted border. Use the brown thread. Make stitches about 1/4 inch apart for decorative purposes.

3. Place sunflower and brown center in position. Pin. Quilt around brown center piece about 1/8 inch in from edge with the light brown thread.

4. For stem, cut 1/4-inch by 3 1/2-inch strip of green fabric. Slip stem under flower. Quilt stem along center with green thread through all thicknesses.

5. For leaves, pin in position. Attach leaves to stem with 2 long stitches. Quilt center veins through all thicknesses.

6. Tie knots in ends of jute string. Sew to hanging at top.

Sunflower Source Guide

Source List for Sunflower Seeds

W. Atlee Burpee & Co.
300 Park Ave.
Warminster, PA 18974
Phone (800) 333-5808
Fax (215) 674-4170

DeGiorgi Seeds & Goods
6011 'N' Street
Omaha, NE 68117-1634
Phone (402) 731-3901

Gurney's Seed & Nursery Co.
110 Capital St.
Yankton, SD 57079
Phone (605) 665-1671
Fax (605) 665-9718

Johnny's Selected Seeds
310 Foss Hill Rd.
Albion, ME 04910-9731
Phone (207) 437-4357
Fax (207) 437-2165

Native Seeds/SEARCH
2509 N. Campbell Ave. #325
Tucson, AZ 85719
Phone (602) 327-9123

Nichols Garden Nursery
1190 North Pacific Highway
Albany, OR 97321-4598
Phone (503) 928-9280
Fax (503) 967-8406

Park Seed
Cokesbury Rd.
Greenwood, SC 29647-0001
Phone (803) 941-4480
Fax (803) 941-4206

Pinetree Garden Seeds
Box 300
New Gloucester, ME 04260
Phone (207) 926-3400
Fax (207) 926-3886

Shepherd's Garden Seeds
30 Irene St.
Torrington, CT 06790
Phone (203) 482-3638

Stokes Seeds Inc.
Box 548
Buffalo, NY 14240-0548
Phone (716) 695-6980
Fax (716) 695-9649

The Cook's Garden
P.O. Box 535
Londonderry, VT 05148
Phone (802) 824-3400
Fax (802) 824-3027

Thompson & Morgan Inc.
P.O. Box 1308
Jackson, NJ 08527-0308
Phone (908) 363-2225
Fax (908) 363-9356

Source List for Maximilian Sunflowers

Wildseed Farms, Inc.
1101 Campo Rosa Road
P.O. Box 308
Eagle Lake, TX 77434-0308
Phone (800) 848-0078
Fax (409) 234-7407

Source List for Jerusalem Artichokes

Burgess Seed & Plant Co.
905 Four Seasons Rd.
Bloomington, IL 61701
Phone (309) 663-9551

Gurneys Seed & Nursery Co.
110 Capital St.
Yankton, SD 57079
Phone (605) 665-1671
Fax (605) 665-9718

Johnny's Selected Seeds
310 Foss Hill Rd.
Albion, ME 04910-9731
Phone (207) 437-4357
Fax (207) 437-2165

Mellinger's
2310 W. South Range Rd.
North Lima, OH 44452-9731
Phone (214) 549-9861
Fax (216) 549-3716

W. Atlee Burpee & Co.
300 Park Ave.
Warminster, PA 18974
Phone (800) 333-5808
Fax (215) 674-4170